Pathways

Kailey Gober

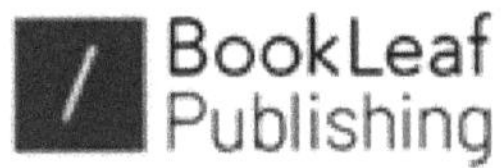

BookLeaf Publishing

Presentation by *BookLeaf Publishing*

Web: www.bookleafpub.com

E-mail: info@bookleafpub.com

ISBN : 9789357699686

First edition 2022

DEDICATION

I dedicate this to my mom, who has always been there for me. And to Kayla and Liz, my amazing best friends who have stuck by my side.

In The Bay Window

Tick Tock.
Pitter Patter.
Rustle,
Flutter. Time going by.
Rain falling.
Moving blanket.
Pages turning.

The Villain

2

Never fall for the hero's charms.
For a hero will never show you his flaws.
They would sacrifice you for the world,
But once you meet the villain you will see his
story.
You will see he's not so full of glory.
He would sacrifice the world for you.
A hero gets fame and gratitude,
Whereas the villain gets fame and hatred.
Never fall for the hero's charms because he is
not all that you think.
But a villain will always be who you seek.

Her

3

She loves the smell of oncoming rain.
She loves the smell that comes after.
The smell of a campfire,
Of burning wood.
When it's lit.
When it's put out.
The smell of rain and fire.
But never flowers.

The Shadows

The shadows they hold lies.
They hold hidden truths.
People hide in the shadows.
And yet...
They all curse the shadows they hide in.

Beauty of the Shadows.

The shadows are dark.
They're mysterious.
But they're also light and airy.
Shadows hold a certain beauty,
They aren't scared of themselves,
Instead they take pride in themselves.
And that is the beauty of shadows.

Look

Look.
Look between the branches.
Watch how the sun filters through.
Bathing the forest in golden light before it hides.
Before the sun dips below the horizon,
Only to let the moon have his turn.
His turn to shine his light.
Painting the leaves and flowers with a silver
shine.
Giving the Earth the illusion of being frosted
over.
All you have to do is look.

Falling

7

They fall.
One by one.
They fall down.
Layering the frosty ground.
Blanketing the world in white,
In the empty silent night.

Ice

8

Pale as snow,
Cold as ice.
Rethink what you know,
They aren't always nice.
Hide your thoughts,
Suppress your fears,
Look what you caught
As your fate draws near.
You're pale as snow.
Heart as cold as ice.
If I would've known...
Well let's just say
You wouldn't be ice.

Dead of Night

In the dead of night is where you lie.
In the dead of night is where you hide.
The demons took you to their side,
You could've at least said goodbye.

Willow Tree

Surrounded by the willow tree
Its branches hanging low.
Surrounded by the willow tree
With its lovely shadow.
Surrounded by the willow tree
Its red and orange leaves bright.
Surrounded by the willow tree
And its ever beautiful sight.

Burning Rose

Do you know what love is?
Love?
It is a burning rose.
Before,
During,
And after it is lit.

Loving Captive

Standing on the edge of the pier
The crashing waves mist and spray her.
The salty water sticks to her tear stained cheeks
Tears that have long since dried.
The wind blows her hair over her face
And blows it behind her too.
Her once bright hazel eyes fill once more with
tears.
She watched as the tide pulled back.
Then she jumps.
Becoming a loving captive of the angry sea.

By Choice

13

In my little boat of solitude in the middle of the
sea,
Looking up at the bright starry sky,
Unaware of the monsters.
The monsters that come up from the deep inky
black depths.
I'm not afraid,
The monsters should be the ones afraid.
Because I'm in the middle of the sea by choice.
It will always be by choice.
And I won't let the monsters ruin that for me.

In The Darkness

Darkness.
Inky black emptiness.
Nothingness,
At least that's what most see,
Actually that's what all see.
All but me.
There is more beauty,
More fulfillment and peace in that inky black
darkness
Then I have ever found in the light.

Whispers

15

Shouts.
They get around.
They get heard,
More than your whispers.
I hear your shouts;
But, I also hear your whispers.
Because the shouts are heard clear as day.
But your whispers hide in the shadows of the
night.

Cerulean Eyes

Deep cerulean eyes.
These eyes pierce through my soul.
They see every lie that passes through my dry
pink lips.
They see when I put up my walls.
Then I wake up...
And I realize he's nothing more than a fictional
character.
A character pulled out of my favorite book and
the deepest crevices of my mind.
A character I wish with all my might was real.
But he's not,
So in my dreams and fantasies is where he'll
stay.
My character.
My person.
With the deep cerulean eyes.

Grey

White.
So bland.
So bright.
Black.
So dark.
So empty.
Grey.
So beautifully soft,
And so perfectly dark.

Temporary

18

Trying so hard to ignore reality.
Book,
After book,
After book.
A way to escape.
That's all she wants.
An escape.
But those escapes are only temporary.
...Always temporary.
But she doesn't want temporary.

Your Place

Through the trees,
High and low branches hide you.
Past the streams,
Swift and cold waters are now behind you.
Over the hill top,
Galaxies above and plush green beneath you.
Through the fields of flowers,
To the place that has always called you.

That Patch of Sand

Sitting on a patch of sand,
Looking up at the crescent moon she sobs and
thinks.
"Don't."
She hums in reply to the voice in her head.
"It'll only hurt;
So don't."
A deep sigh leaves her rosy lips.
She knows it's true,
So she pulls her knees up to her chest laying her
chin on top.
Staring longingly at the silver crescent moon,
Sitting on that patch of sand.

Part of the Stars

There are days when she thinks too much.
But those thoughts always lead to one painful
wish,
One painful nightmare.
She dreams of lying down,
Looking up at the sky;
A beautiful starry night sky.
As she lays there she sees a shooting star.
Closing her eyes she makes a wish.
She wishes to join the other stars up in the night
sky.

She takes her last deep breath.
Exhales.
Closing her eyes for the last time.
When she opens them again she's looking down.
At that moment she can't help but be happy;
Her wish came true.
Now she's part of the stars.

Ingram Content Group UK Ltd.
Milton Keynes UK
UKHW020745070623
423023UK00015B/782